I don't want to get up.
If
AND DO THINGS.
Noooo...

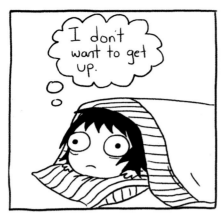

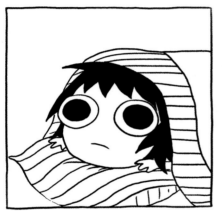

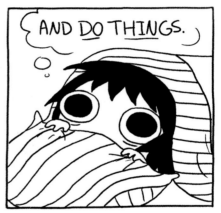

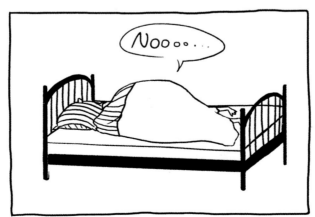

I SHOULD BE:

I AM:

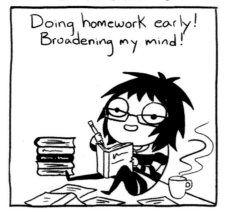

Doing homework early!
Broadening my mind!

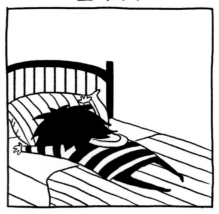

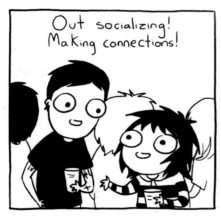

Out socializing!
Making connections!

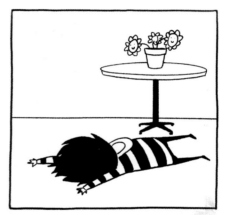

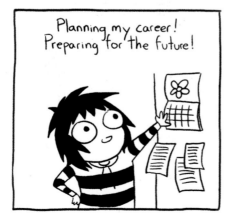

Planning my career!
Preparing for the future!

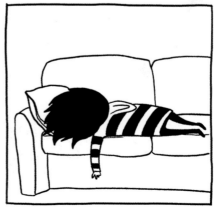

ADULTHOOD
IS A MYTH

A "Sarah's Scribbles" collection

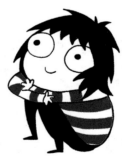

Sarah Andersen

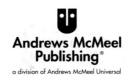

Andrews McMeel Publishing®

a division of Andrews McMeel Universal

Z

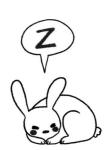

WRITTEN COMMUNICATION

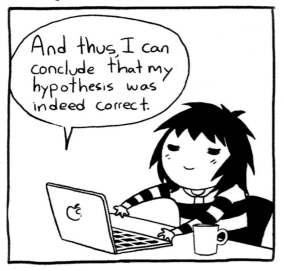

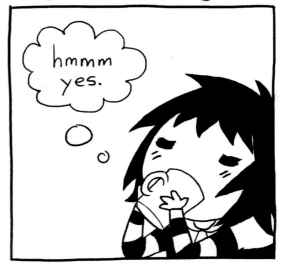

VERBAL COMMUNICATION

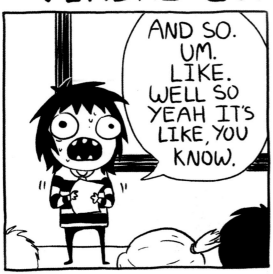

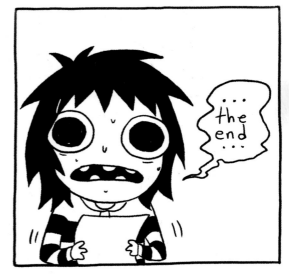

NIGHTMARES FOR INTROVERTS

1) Sales people
Hi! I'm about to make your shopping experience super uncomfortable!
2) Restaurants with no online takeout
Hello... Yes, no, um —what? Oh, I...
3) Being on the outside of a conversation circle
4) This question
Why are you so quiet?

LOOK AT THIS.
Look, you're always perfect to me. And you should love yourself no matter what.
No, look. I can make it talk.
MNEH MNEH MNEH

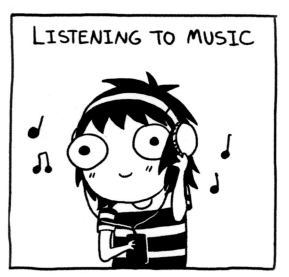

LISTENING TO MUSIC

REALIZING THE ARTIST IS YOUNGER THAN YOU

GETTING DRESSED

Decent wardrobe
...
Five-year-old ratty sweater stolen from my dad
...

HEY.
Hi.
He spoke to me...

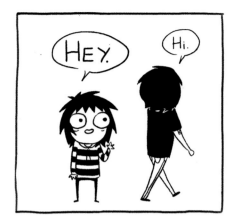

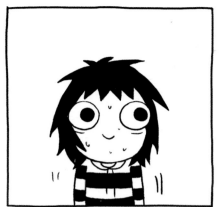

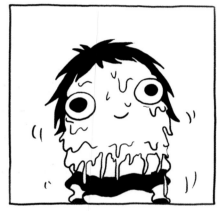

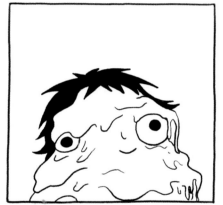

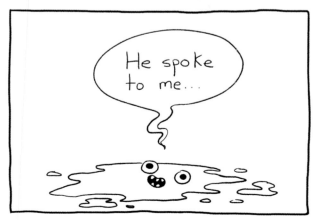

I feel pretty today.
Wow, okay, nevermind.

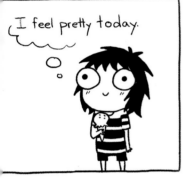

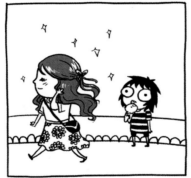

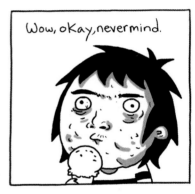

WHEN TO CHANGE/WASH

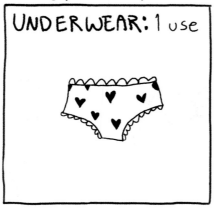

UNDERWEAR: 1 use

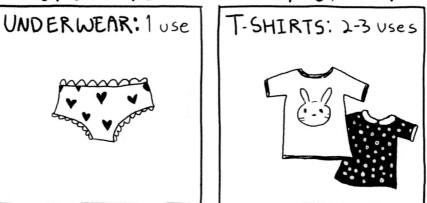

T-SHIRTS: 2-3 uses

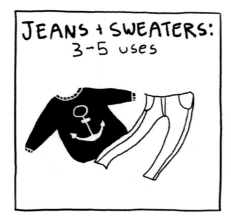

JEANS + SWEATERS: 3-5 uses

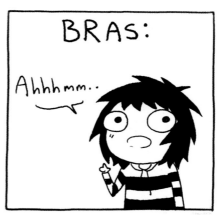

BRAS:

Ahhhmm..

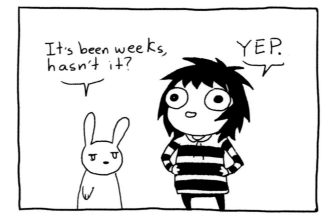

It's been weeks, hasn't it?

YEP.

MAKING FRIENDS

1) Find someone you enjoy talking to.

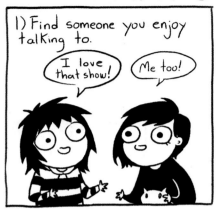

2) Exchange contact info.

3) Despite contrary evidence, assume they dislike you.

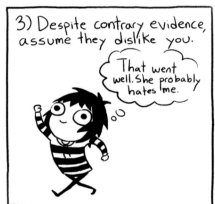

4) Based on this assumption, never contact them first.

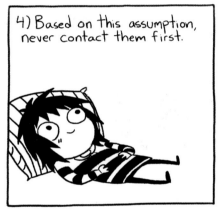

5) Die alone.

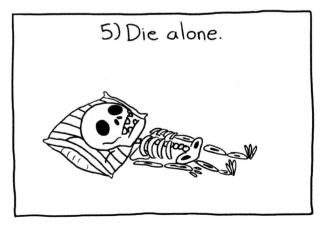

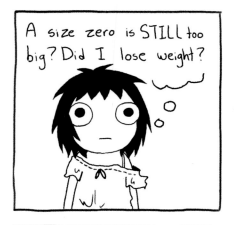

A size zero is STILL too big? Did I lose weight?

LATER, IN ANOTHER DRESSING ROOM...

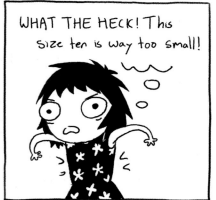

WHAT THE HECK! This size ten is way too small!

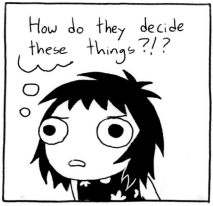

How do they decide these things?!?

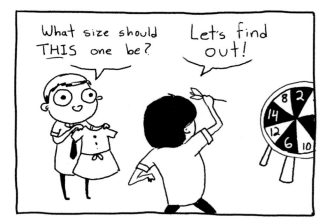

What size should THIS one be?

Let's find out!

STILL NO BABY?!
Stomach
Uterus
NNNNGGHH

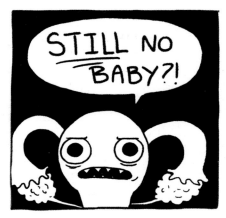

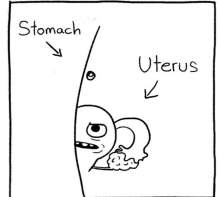

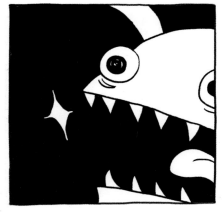

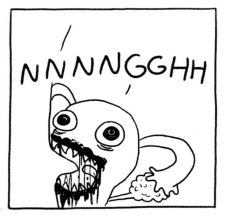

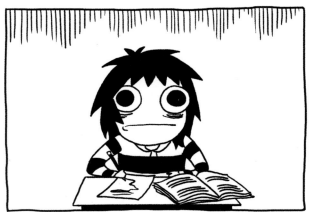

GOING BACK TO SCHOOL

I HATE YOU.
Heyyy
HATE YOU, TOO.
Welcome back.
Thanks.
ESPECIALLY hate you...
ohmigosh HHEEEYYY
And you. And you. And you.
YUP. I HATE ALL OF YOU.

I have an awful headache!
Drink water.
My stomach hurts.
Drink water.
I'm having emotional issues.
Drink water.
MY LEG IS BROKE-
Drink water.
-MUFFLED SCREAMING-
Drink water!

DATING

Well, I grew up
I KNOW.
And then I went to school in...
I KNOW
I KNOW EVERYTHING ABOUT YOU.
I HAVE BEEN THROUGH YOUR ENTIRE FACEBOOK AND TWITTER HISTORY.
And that's how I wound up here!
Interesting.

MANICURE

TWO DAYS LATER:
Sigh.

PEDICURE

50 YEARS LATER:
Your toes look nice, Gramma.
Thanks. I did them when I was 22.

MAN.
I love books.
Uh, your book is upside down.
I know, I just love the smell.
SNNNFFFF
Knowledge.

I hate my generation.
I'm not like THOSE girls.
Top 40? You guys should try listening to REAL music.
UGH. PREPS.
THE SPECIAL SNOWFLAKE CLUB
YOU'RE ALL BABIES!

Ooooh, you draw?
YUP.

Will you draw me-
NOPE.

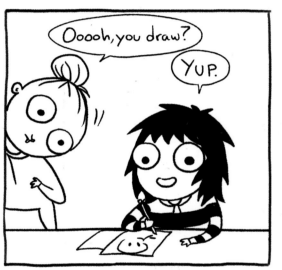

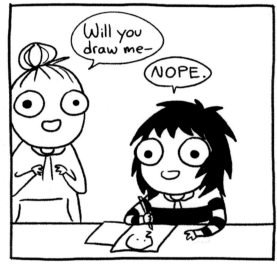

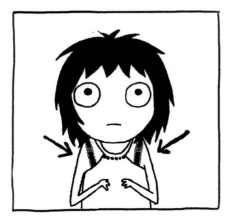

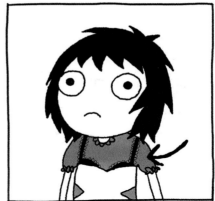

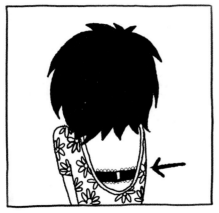

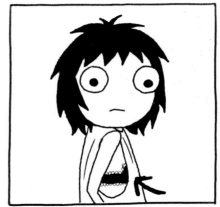

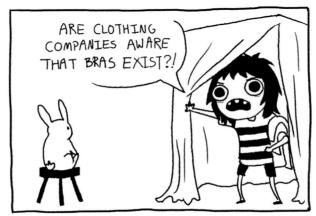

ARE CLOTHING COMPANIES AWARE THAT BRAS EXIST?!

PROCRASTINATION

PHEW.
I did the dishes, scrubbed the floors, dusted, did the laundry...
...PLUS I organized all the—
How's the paper?

SHAMPOO VS. CONDITIONER

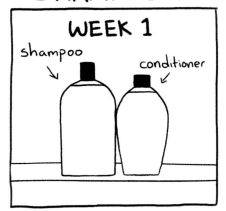

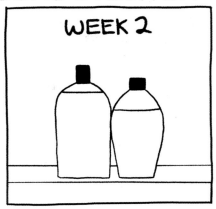

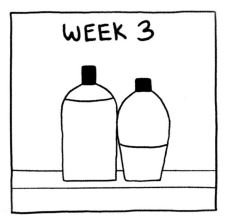

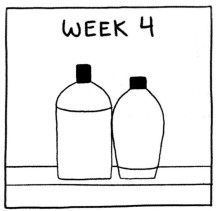

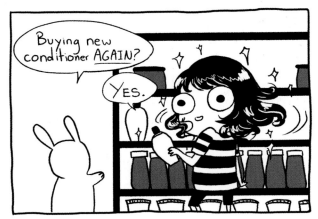

THE UGLY SHOE TREND

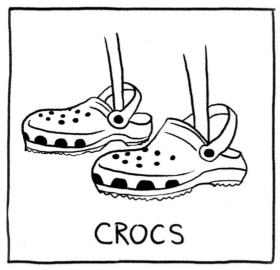

CROCS

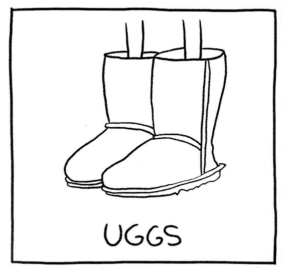

UGGS

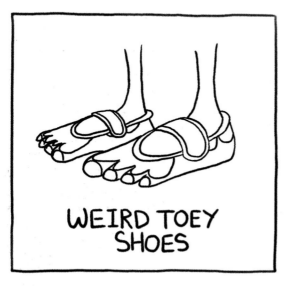

WEIRD TOEY SHOES

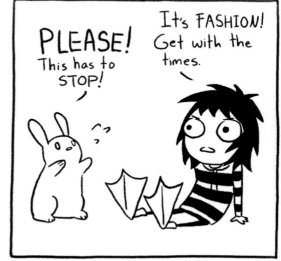

NOTEBOOKS

EXPECTATION:

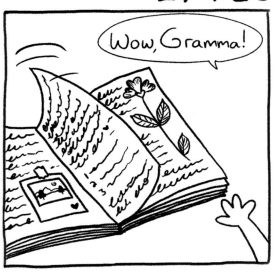

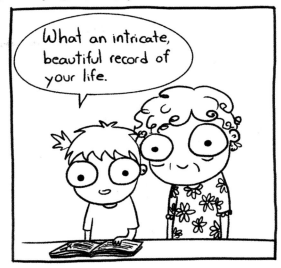

REALITY:

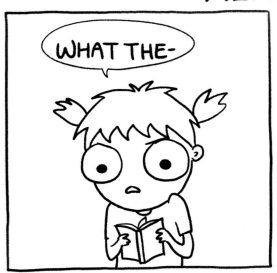

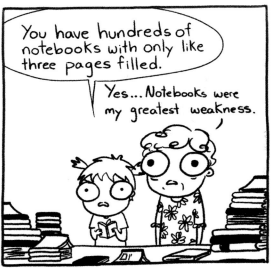

HOLDING HANDS

OKAY OKAY. I'm just gonna go for it.
DING
MY HAND IS SWEATY.
Oh no
Oh god
He thinks I'm gross oh god oh god oh god oh god...
WHAT IS THIS HELL?

GIRL'S PURSE

That'll be ten dollars.
Sure, let me just find-
...HM.
Wh-
Where am I?

Z
GASP
It's 3:00 AM!
It's high time for me to stand on my owner for no reason!!!
MROW.

ME AGE 13
oh god, what if I missed a leg hair when I shaved, oh no oh no.
ME NOW
I HOPE YOU'RE READY FOR ME, WORLD.

I like you.
What? Really?
Yeah!
You're sure you like me?
I do.
So you won't change your mind?
Nah.
You don't think I'm weird?
Nope.
So you definitely like me-
YES.
RIP
RIP

THINGS I KNOW

The yellow fever virus was the first human virus ever discovered.

Humans have around 70,000 thoughts a day.

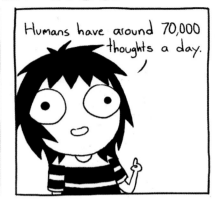

Kepler-186f is an Earth-size planet that is located in the "habitable zone" of its star.

A clam named Ming lived to be 507.

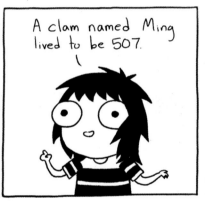

THINGS I DON'T KNOW

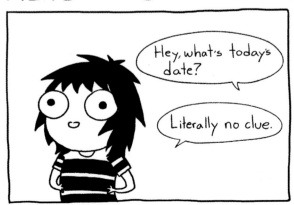

Hey, what's today's date?

Literally no clue.

Oh man. You look tired.
Yeah.
You okay? You look tired.
Uh huh.
You tired?
Wow.
You look tired.
You look super duper tired.
THAT'S BECAUSE I AM TIRED.
So that's why!
Ooooohhh
Makes sense.

"SYNCING"

Oh! Hey again!
Hey!
I've been seeing you around a lot lately!
We should try to meet up more often!
Totally!
Maybe sometime later this month?
LATER THAT MONTH:

So. How are finals going?

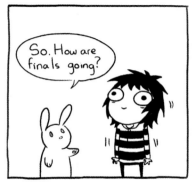

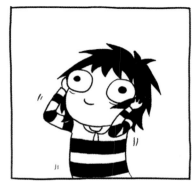

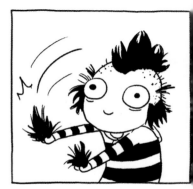

HOW I CLEAN MY ROOM

HNG.
Ahhh.
I did good.

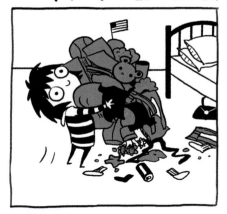

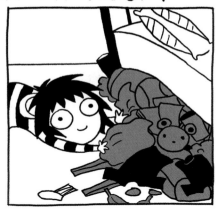

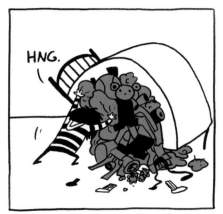

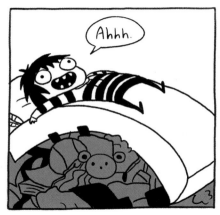

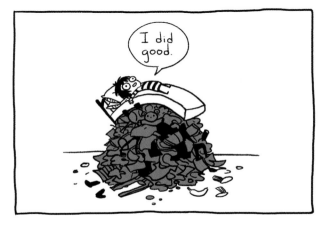

I'm not going to buy this dress, it's too small...
HNG.
I'm stuck.
HNNNNGGG
I'm going to die like this, aren't I...

I look AMAZING in these heels!
You can't move, can you.
Not at all.

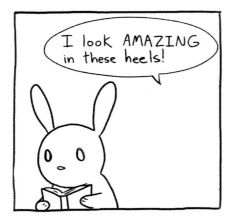

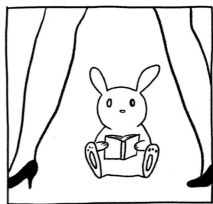

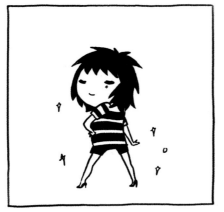

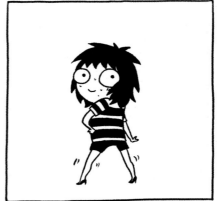

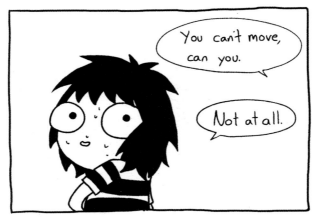

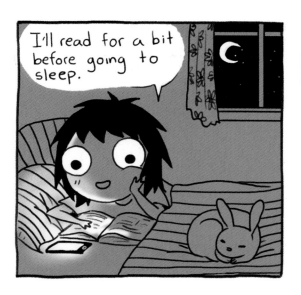

I'll read for a bit before going to sleep.

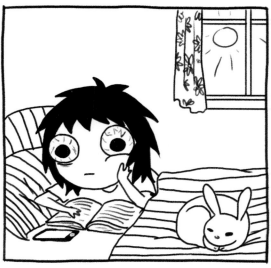

ADVICE

...And that's not all! He's AWFUL!
I think maybe you need to break up.
He seems like he's making you unhappy.
You know, you're right.
LATER:
Instagram
LUV U BBY!!!!

REAL girls don't—
WAIT! STOP!
Do you identify as a girl?
Yes.
Are you a figment of my imagination?
No.
CONGRATULATIONS!
You have met the criteria for being a REAL girl!
Why do you have confetti?

HABITS OF THE COMMON BOOKWORM

1) Mispronouncing words because you've only ever read them.

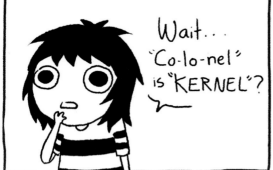

Wait... "Co-lo-nel" is "KERNEL"?

2) Ability to maneuver crowds without looking up.

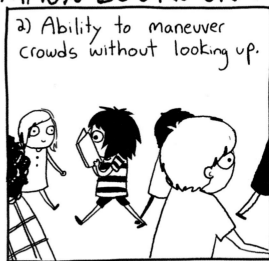

3) A particular affinity for the smell of ink and paper.

This should be a perfume.

4) Building cozy nests for reading.

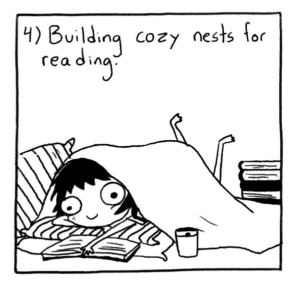

41

SLOW WALKERS

I'M LATE I'M LATE
I'M LATE I'M LATE
Oop.
And so then I was like...
Come on guys... A little faster.
And she was all...
Go go go go go
GO GO GO GO
GO GO
GOOOOOOOo
What's she doing?

THINGS I COULD DO
WHEN MY WIFI IS DOWN

1) Read a book.

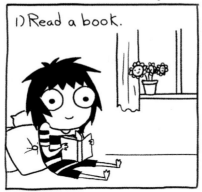

2) Enjoy the weather.

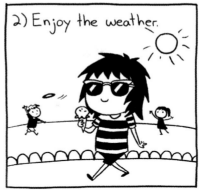

3) Catch up with a friend.

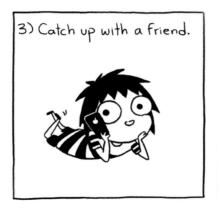

4) Clean and organize.

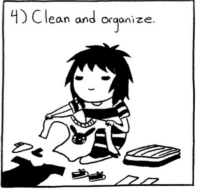

WHAT I DO

Spend hours doing this:

CONNECT
YOU STUPID
SONOFA—

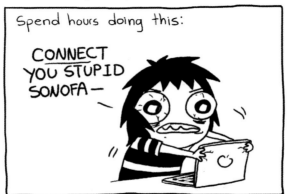

43

I AM SO STRESSED!!
Meditate?
I just have SO much to do...
Make a list?
...And I have NO time...
Well, Maybe you should-
STOP TRYING TO HELP, I'M TRYING TO COMPLAIN HERE!

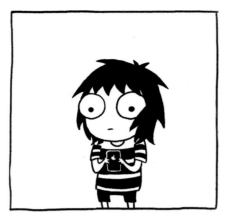

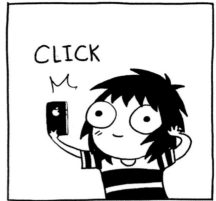

CLICK

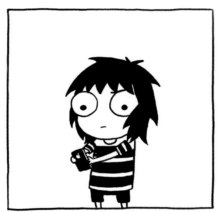

Ah, yes. There they are.

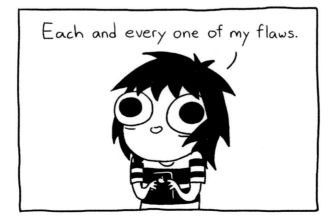

Each and every one of my flaws.

GETTING DRUNK (For Beginners)

1) Have a drink.

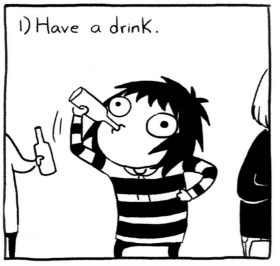

2) Tell everyone you're drunk.

HAHAHA I'M SO DRUNK.

YOOOOO

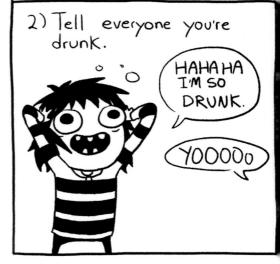

3) Tell <u>EVERYONE</u> you're drunk.

OMg I had a beer LOL I am sOoOo WASTED!111

Haha?

Okay.

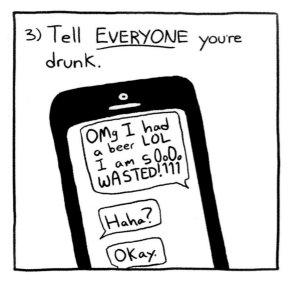

4) Discuss.

I am drunk!

GURL me too!

I, too, am drunk.

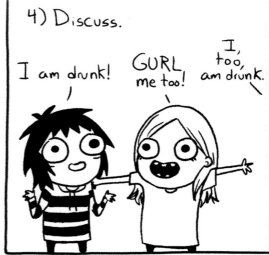

NORMAL PEOPLE
It appears my hamper is full.
I can thus conclude that it is time to do laundry.
ME
SNNNF
Well, all the shirts in my clothing pile smell funny, so...

CLEANING TIPS

1) Donate clothes that don't fit.

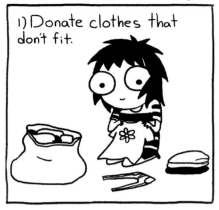

2) Clean out expired cosmetics.

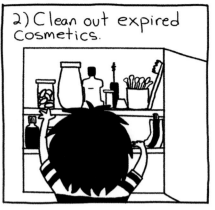

3) Get rid of old—

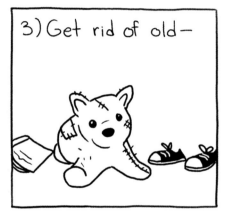

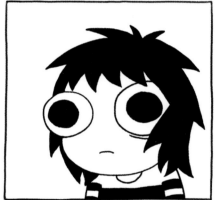

Do not, under any circumstances, get rid of old stuffed animals.

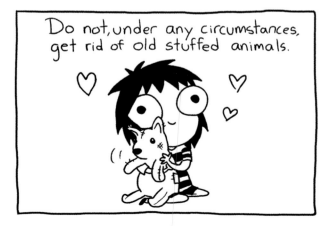

What the... where am I?
Your time has come! We must now review your life.
Neat!
We'll start with your internet search history.
You know what? I'm out.
But-
I'll just head over to limbo.

BAD RELATIONSHIP

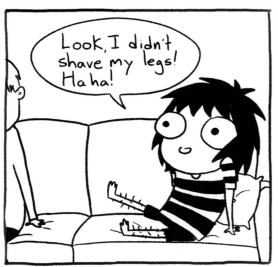

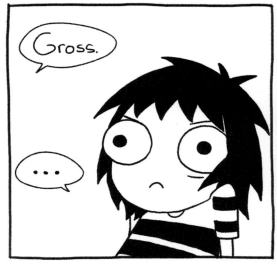

GOOD RELATIONSHIP

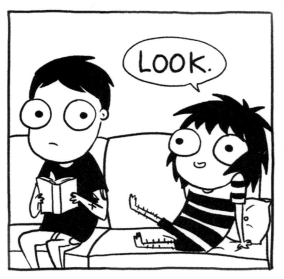

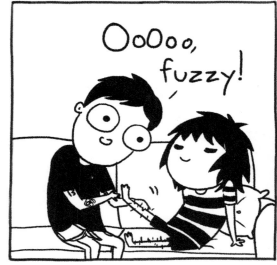

ME IN THE FUTURE

And this is what I looked like as a teen!
Here's another one.
...And another.
...And about 10,000 more.
FLIP
PHOTO
Jesus Christ, Gramma.
Yeah... I took a lot of selfies.

SOCIAL MEDIA IN REAL LIFE

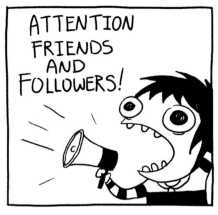

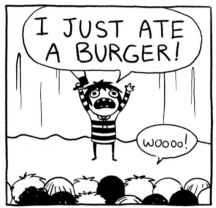

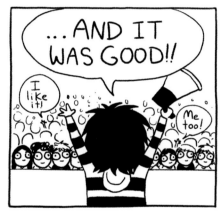

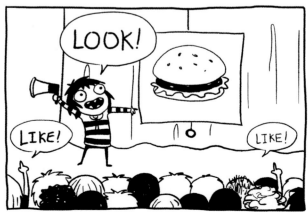

GOD. I feel so DEPRESSED.
What? What's wrong?
Nothing. Literally nothing.
I don't get it.
But I'm so SAD.
What's wrong with me? What could it BE?
ELSEWHERE:
TWO MORE DAYS...

MASSAGES FOR REGULAR PEOPLE

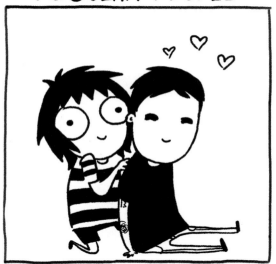

MASSAGES FOR TICKLISH PEOPLE

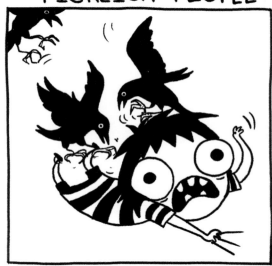

I just read five pages without absorbing a single word.

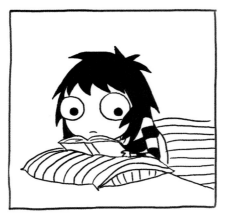

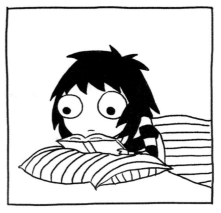

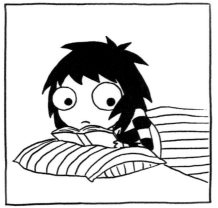

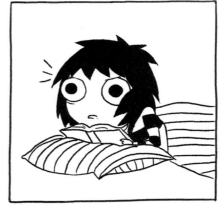

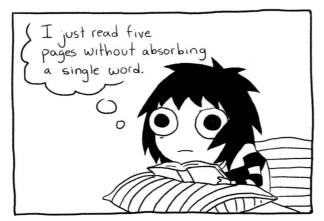

WHAT I EAT ON A TYPICAL DAY

1) Bowl of cereal

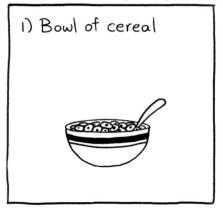

2) Simple lunch

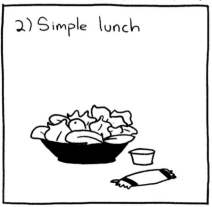

3) Slice of pizza

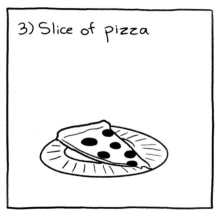

4) Tons and tons of snacks I absentmindedly eat and totally forget about

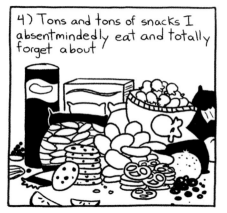

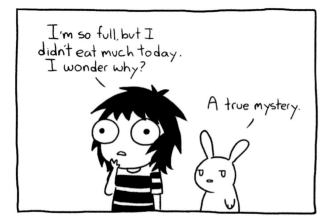

Oh hey. It's October!
I KNOW.

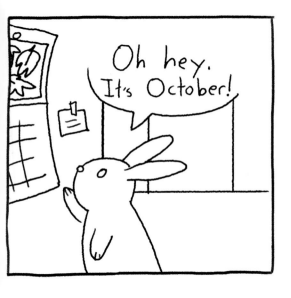

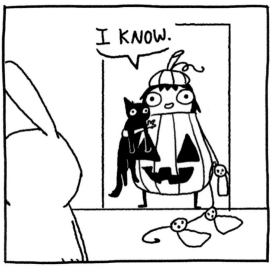

see ya later!
SMOOCH
What the...What's covering my eyes?
I CAN'T SEE!
I'M BLIND!
You're in love.

SOCIALLY UNACCEPTABLE

Hairy armpits on girls

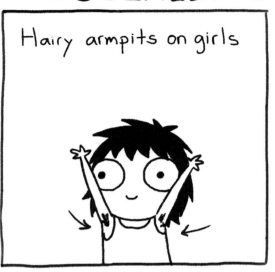

Hairy legs on girls

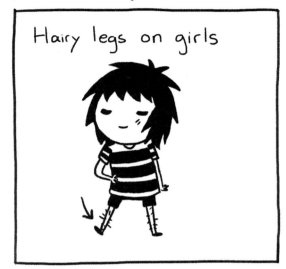

SOCIALLY ACCEPTABLE

Thin, sweaty, pimply, creepy caterpillar mustaches

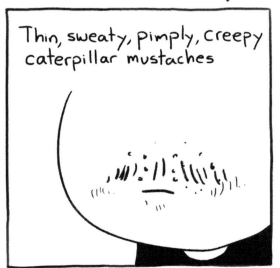

THIS IS AN UNJUST WORLD!

5 PHRASES THAT MAKE
MY BLOOD RUN COLDER THAN ICE

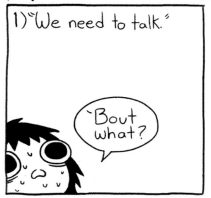

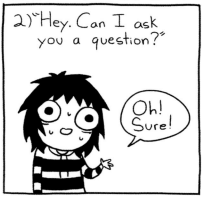

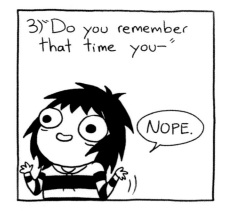

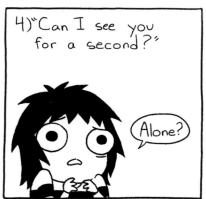

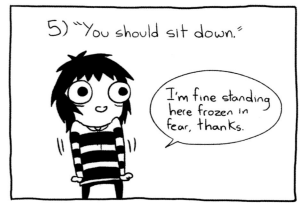

WATCHING STUFF

NEW RELATIONSHIP:

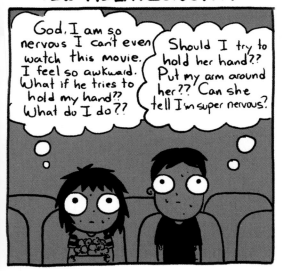

LONG-TERM RELATIONSHIP:

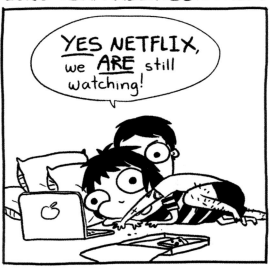

EXERCISE
Pros:

1) Increased muscle mass

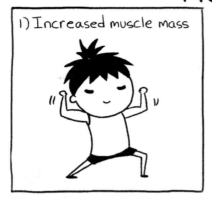

2) Better mood

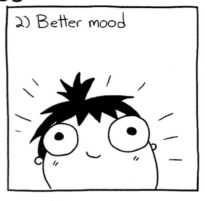

3) More energy

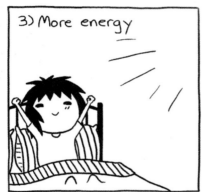

4) Better heart health and strength

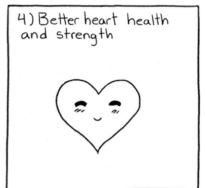

Cons:

1) Exercising

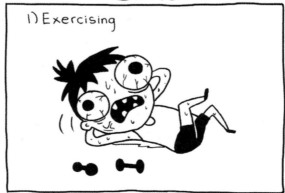

OoOo. These are cute.
SALE
I'm gonna get 'em.
Enjoy them while they last.

I need to get my eyebrows done!
Push your bangs back. Let me see.

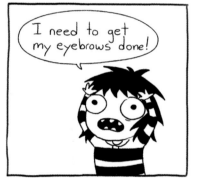

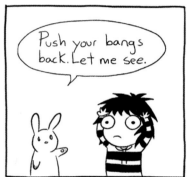

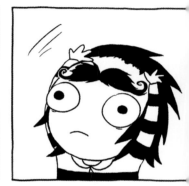

I can't wait to go home and change into my pajamas.
I can't wait to go home and change into my pajamas.
HO
I can't wait to go home and change into my pajamas.
I can't wait to go home and change into my pajamas.
I'm so happy I'm home and in my pajamas.

Hey. Could I look through your sketchbook?
sure.
Excuse me while I go have an emotional, artistic, and existential crisis.
what?

THINGS THAT MAKE ME FEEL SAFE

1) Leaving the TV on

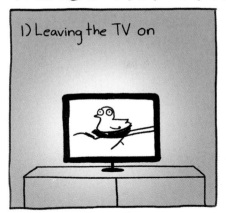

2) Being under the covers

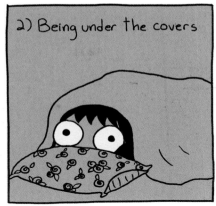

3) Leaving the bathroom light on

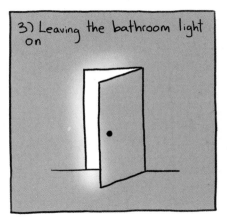

4) Having the cat in the room

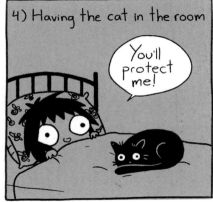

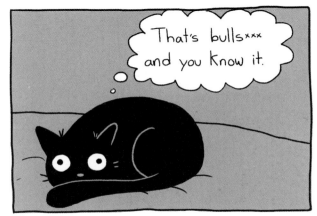

HOW TO ENJOY A RAINY DAY

1) Find a cuddle buddy

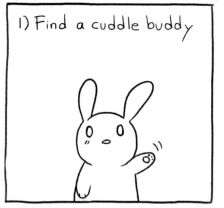

2) A hot drink

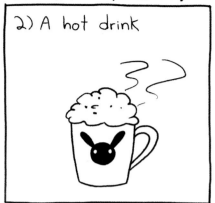

3) A good movie

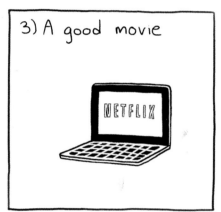

4) A blanket pile

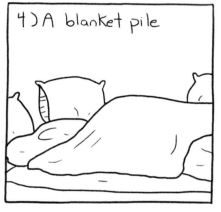

5) Enjoy being the coziest human ever.

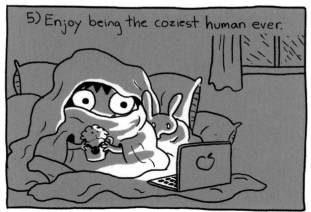

sketching
Hey.
That arm is weird. You should redraw it.
I.
DID NOT.
ASK. YOU.

Hey, can you—
Do not disrupt me. I am creating vivid music videos in my head.

ME AGE 13

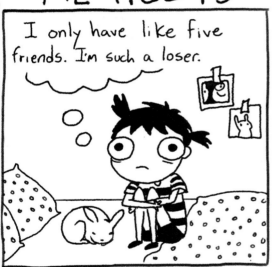

I only have like five friends. I'm such a loser.

ME NOW

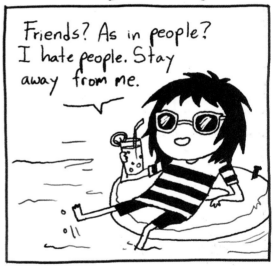

Friends? As in people? I hate people. Stay away from me.

I'm so cozy.
Yeah!
We should just stay like this for the rest of our lives.
Yeah!
50 YEARS LATER
That was a nice life.
Yeah!

WHY I'M ALWAYS LATE
IN THE WINTER

1) Don't wanna leave my warm bed.

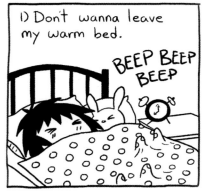

2) Don't wanna leave my warm pajamas.

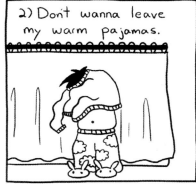

3) Don't wanna leave the warm shower.

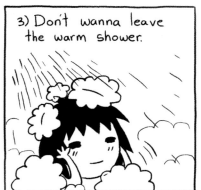

4) Don't wanna leave the warm house.

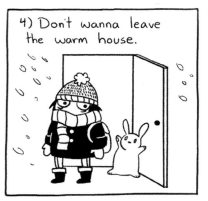

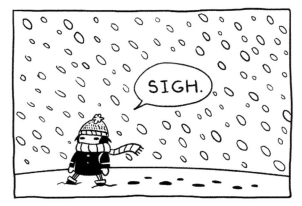

LACY BRAS
PROS:

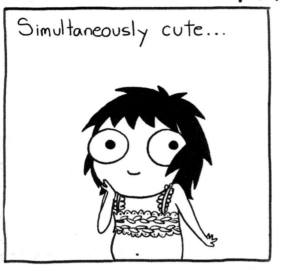

Simultaneously cute...

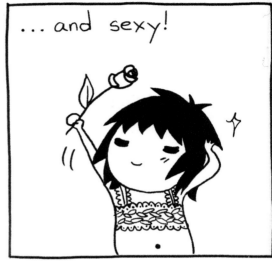

... and sexy!

CONS:

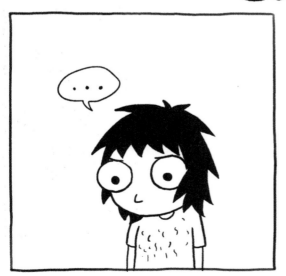

...

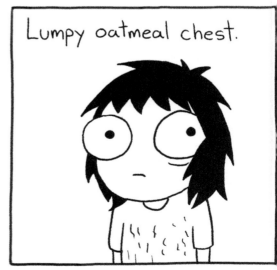

Lumpy oatmeal chest.

BENEFITS OF STEALING BOYS' HOODIES

1) Comfortable and warm.

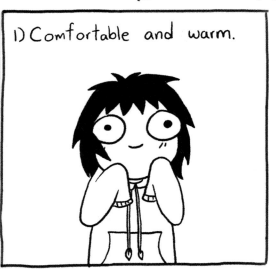

2) Instant shelter.

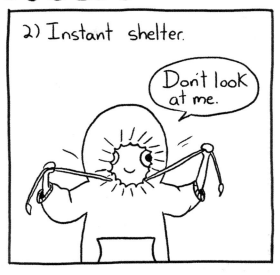

3) Adequate pockets.

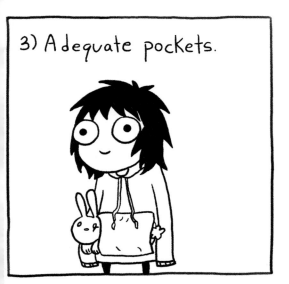

4) The arm flappy thing.

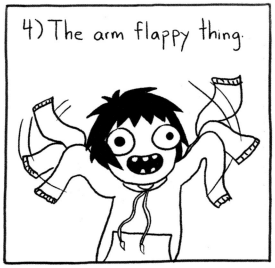

GETTING PAID

Wow. This is so much money.
This is HUNDREDS.
I can buy things worth HUNDREDS of dollars.
I CAN DO ANYTHING!
TWO DAYS LATER:
That was way less money than I thought it was.
Mhm.
RAMEN

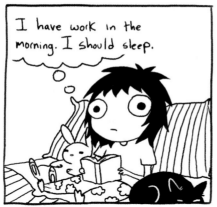

I have work in the morning. I should sleep.

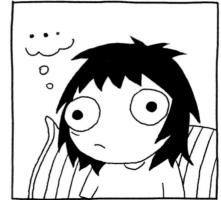

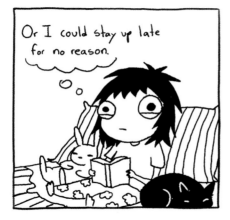

Or I could stay up late for no reason.

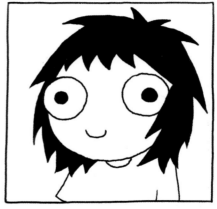

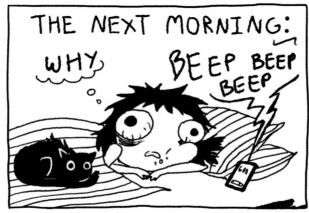

THE NEXT MORNING:

WHY

BEEP BEEP BEEP

NORMAL PEOPLE
I can't believe that happened. How embarrassing!
TWO MINUTES LATER:
Ehh... Oh well.
SHRUG
ME
I AM SO EMBARRASSED.
ON MY DEATH BED:
I can't believe I did that thing 60 years ago...

GIVING GIFTS

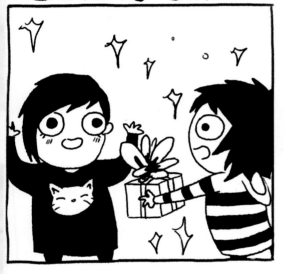

RECEIVING GIFTS

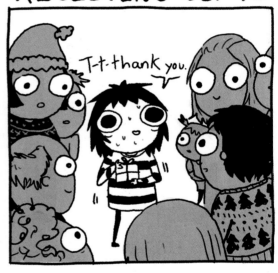

T-t-thank you.

ME BEFORE THE HOLIDAYS

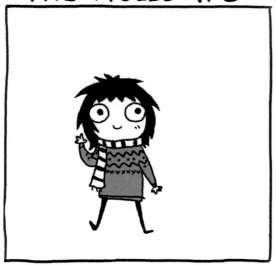

ME AFTER THE HOLIDAYS

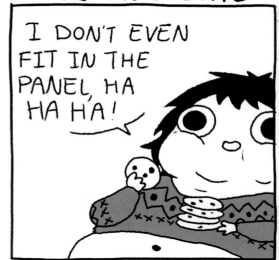

Check out this new hot top 40 single!
This SUCKS.
Oh. Don't worry. You'll learn to like it.
Because I'm gonna play it every day. Everywhere. Over and over and over and over and over.
BUT–
Shhh. Do not be afraid to love.

HOW GRADUATING FEELS

I DONT KNOW IF I CAN DO THIS!!
You'll be fiiiiiiiine.
VRRRRRRR
I'M REALLY SCARED! I'M NOT READY!
Are you sure the back up parachute works?
No clue.
Wait, wha–
WAAAAAAAAAAAAA

AGE 5
I DON'T LIKE BABIES.
Quiet, dear.
AGE 15
I just don't want Kids.
You'll change your mind.
You're young and naive.
AGE 25
Still don't want em!
CHILDREN ARE LITTLE MIRACLES.
AGE 45
YOUR BIOLOGICAL CLOCK IS TICKING.
Too bad!
AGE 85
Aren't you so miserable and alone and sad and filled with regret?
Nah, shutup.

INTERNET COMMENT THREADS

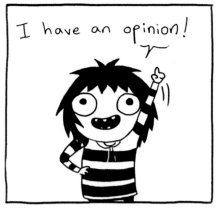

I have an opinion!

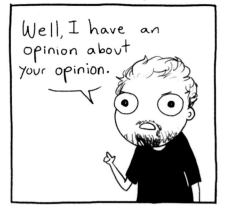

Well, I have an opinion about your opinion.

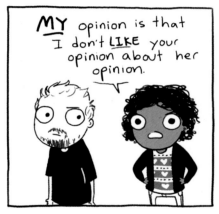

MY opinion is that I don't LIKE your opinion about her opinion.

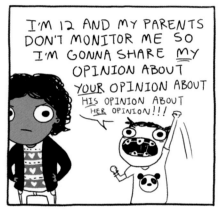

I'M 12 AND MY PARENTS DON'T MONITOR ME SO I'M GONNA SHARE MY OPINION ABOUT YOUR OPINION ABOUT HIS OPINION ABOUT HER OPINION!!!

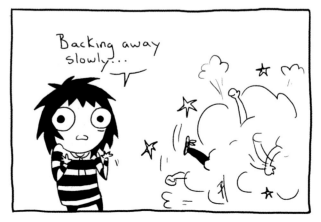

Backing away slowly...

TOMORROW I WILL WAKE UP EARLY!!
THE NEXT DAY:
I did not wake up early.

65° in September

-trying so hard to pretend it's fall-

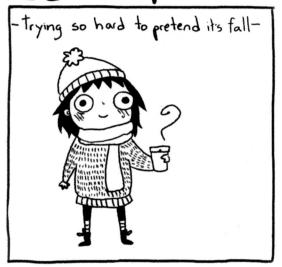

65° in April

-trying so hard to pretend it's summer-

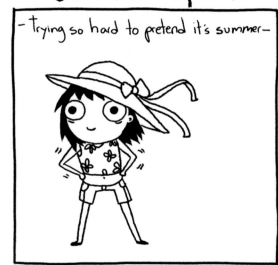

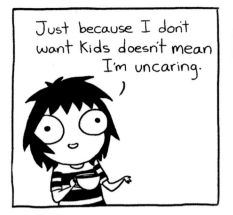

Just because I don't want kids doesn't mean I'm uncaring.

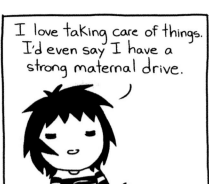

I love taking care of things. I'd even say I have a strong maternal drive.

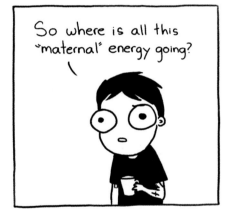

So where is all this "maternal" energy going?

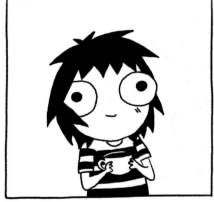

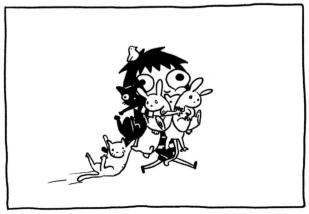

Man. I am so upset.
Do you want a stiff, uncomfortable hug?
Um, I–
Do you feel bette–
–No.

RUNNING INTO PEOPLE YOU KNEW IN HIGH SCHOOL

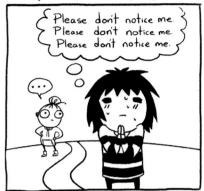

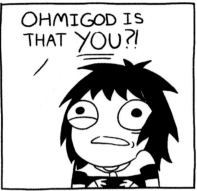

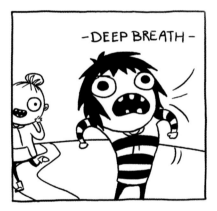

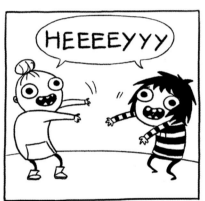

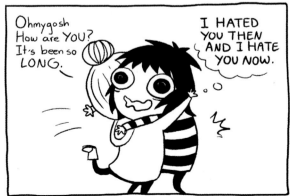

I wanna buy this thing.
Do you need it?
No.
Can you afford it?
No.
Will it have any real, tangible, positive impact on your life or the lives of those around you?
Nooooo...
LATER:
I BOUGHT IT.
WHAP

Now that it's summer, I have time to do the things I'm PASSIONATE about.
Z

RING!
RING!
RING!
HEY, I'M IN A SUPER CROWDED ROOM AND CAN'T PICK UP . . .
FRAUD!

Oh hey! A super important email. I should respond...
LATER ♫
Two weeks later:
Did you ever get to that email?
NOPE.

I'M STRESSED.
You should stop worrying so much.
Wow, thank you! My problem is solved.
Who knew the answer was so SIMPLE?!
I WISH YOU TOLD ME THAT YEARS AGO! I'D BE SO MUCH HAPPIER!
I sense sarcasm.

BANGS IN THE WINTER

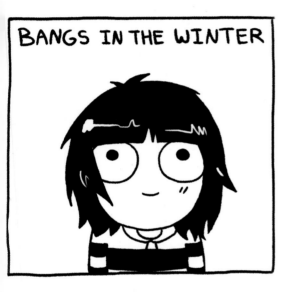

BANGS IN THE SUMMER

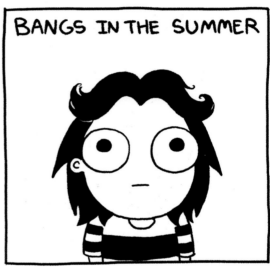

ARTISTS BEING FRIENDS
WITH ARTISTS
Pros:

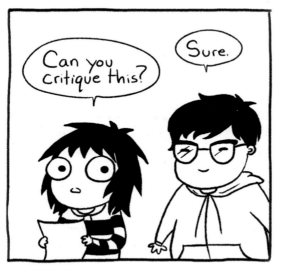

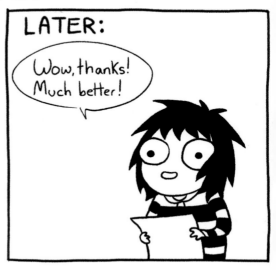

Cons:

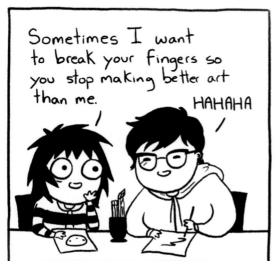

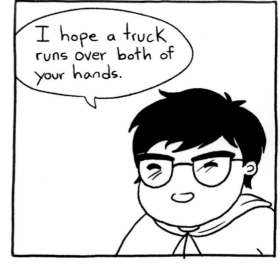

FOLDING LAUNDRY

1) Retrieve laundry.

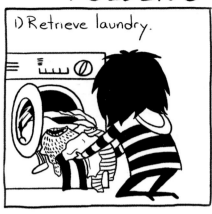

2) Feel the warmth of the laundry.

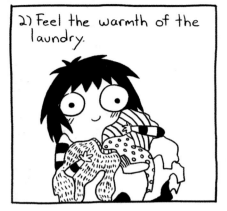

3) Lie in the warmth.

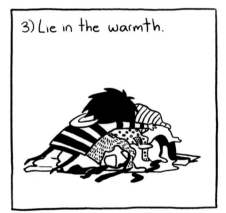

4) . . .

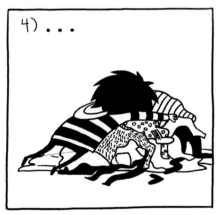

5) Forget the "folding" part.

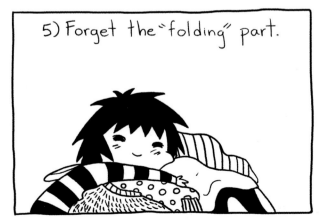

I just worked for fifteen minutes, I DESERVE to watch YouTube.
I haven't spent a lot lately, I DESERVE to splurge.
I had a healthy breakfast, I DESE-
I don't think you know what it means to "deserve" something!
I do not DESERVE this negativity.

WHEN SOMEONE MAKES YOU LAUGH WHEN YOU'RE MAD

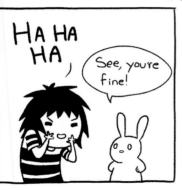

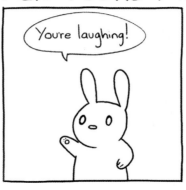

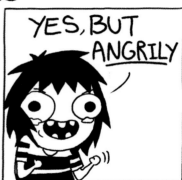

WHEN I'M ON MY PERIOD

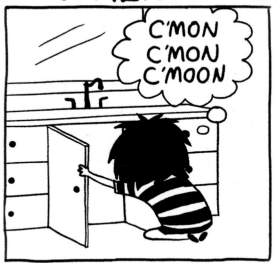

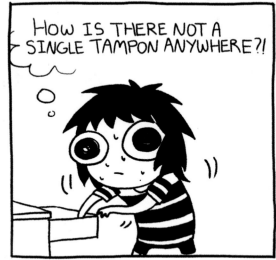

WHEN I'M NOT ON MY PERIOD

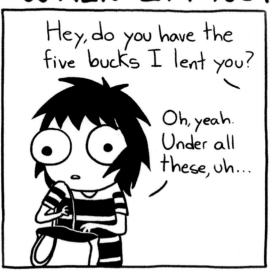

Someone tagged you in a photo!
SLAM

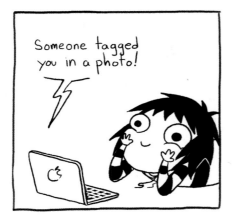

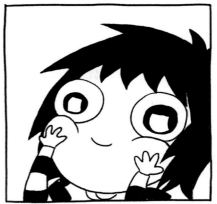

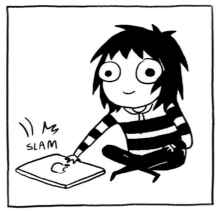

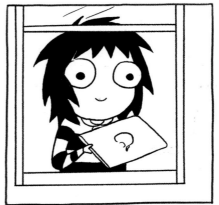

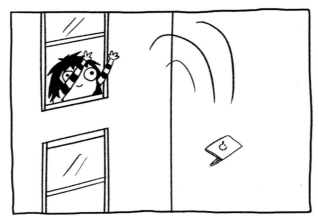

THE INTROVERT'S BRAIN

I wanna talk to people!
But only for a few minutes.
And then I want to go home and recharge in isolation for a whole day.
Sigh.

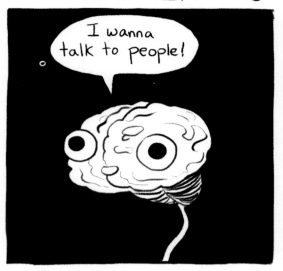

HOW TO KNOW YOUR PARTNER IS SERIOUS ABOUT THE FUTURE

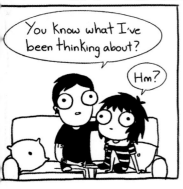

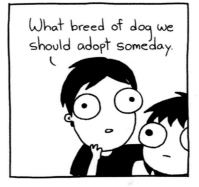

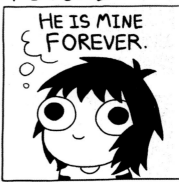

Do not buy those.
99¢
Don't open them.
DO NOT PUT ONE IN YOUR MOUTH.
PLEASE STOP.
YOUR BODY IS A TEMPLE.

REMEMBERING NAMES

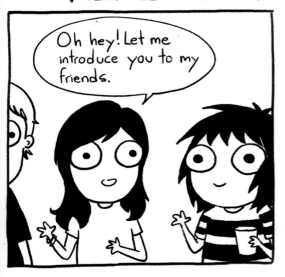

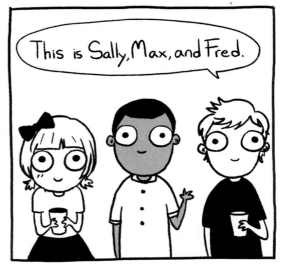

FIVE

SECONDS

LATER

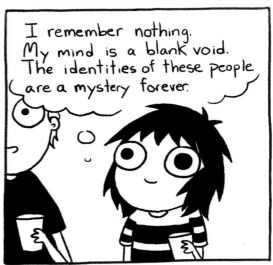

LONG HAIR

EXPECTATION:

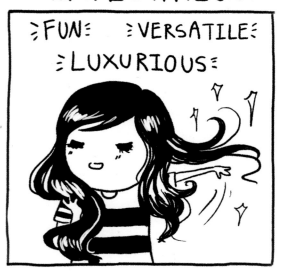

REALITY:

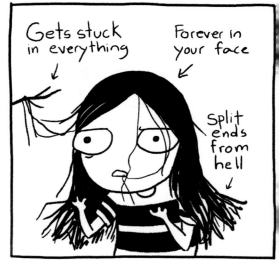

SHORT HAIR

EXPECTATION:

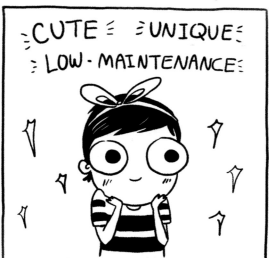

REALITY:

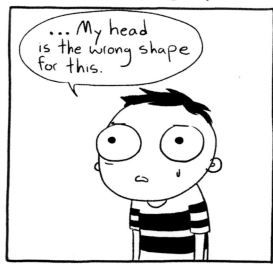

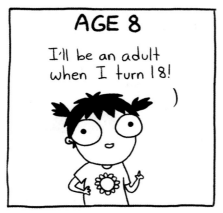

AGE 8

I'll be an adult when I turn 18!

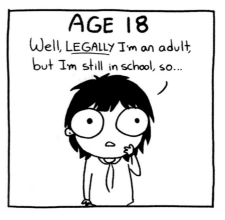

AGE 18

Well, LEGALLY I'm an adult, but I'm still in school, so...

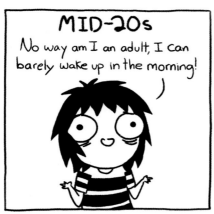

MID-20s

No way am I an adult, I can barely wake up in the morning!

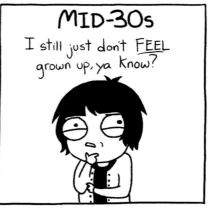

MID-30s

I still just don't FEEL grown up, ya know?

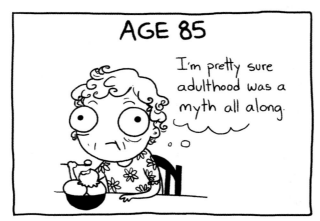

AGE 85

I'm pretty sure adulthood was a myth all along.

So. What are your hobbies?
Um...uh...oh! Well, I go on Wikipedia.
And I'll read an interesting page and follow the links to OTHER cool pages...
...Then I'll read those! I could do it all day!
...
Is that not a valid hobby?

THE FUTURE

So! You'll be an adult soon.

YUP! PSYCHED.

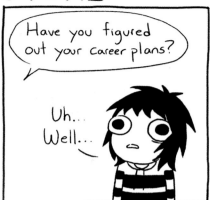

Have you figured out your career plans?

Uh... Well...

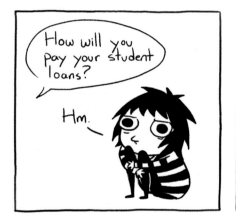

How will you pay your student loans?

Hm.

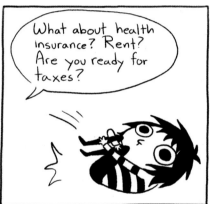

What about health insurance? Rent? Are you ready for taxes?

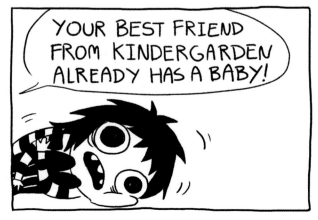

YOUR BEST FRIEND FROM KINDERGARDEN ALREADY HAS A BABY!

ADULTHOOD
IS A MYTH

Andrews McMeel Publishing
a division of Andrews McMeel Universal
1130 Walnut Street, Kansas City, Missouri 64106

www.andrewsmcmeel.com

16 17 18 19 20 TEN 10 9 8 7 6 5 4

ISBN: 978-1-4494-7419-5

Library of Congress Control Number: 2015945439

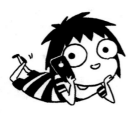

Editor: Grace Suh
Art director and designer: Diane Marsh
Production editor: Erika Kuster
Production manager: Tamara Haus

ATTENTION: SCHOOLS AND BUSINESSES
Andrews McMeel books are available at quantity discounts with
bulk purchase for educational, business, or sales promotional use.
For information, please e-mail the Andrews McMeel Publishing
Special Sales Department: specialsales@amuniversal.com.